OUTSTANDING
MINDSET

HOW TO SET YOURSELF AND YOUR RESTAURANT UP FOR SUCCESS EACH DAY!

DONALD BURNS
THE RESTAURANT COACH™

DISCLAIMER

EXPLICIT LANGUAGE

Author's Note: If you are sensitive to language, then you might want to stop here. The material in this booklet is written in real-world terms and language that occurs in restaurants.

Please note *that I* don't use profanity *to* offend anyone. *I* use *language to* break your thinking patterns *and make* you uncomfortable. When you *get to that place,* then *(and* only then) *will* you *start taking action to change.*

That being said, I have worked in restaurants and kitchens for over nearly four decades and yes, I do drop the F-Bomb quite often. Let's have a fucking great time getting you the restaurant and life you know deep down that you want. See, I warned you.

DEDICATION

To those that want more.

*"We are the music-makers and we
are the dreamers of dreams."*

– Arthur O'Shaughnessy

TABLE OF CONTENTS

INTRODUCTION

I can't encourage you enough to take the time to read this. The principles, techniques, and concepts you will learn in this booklet are proven to work. Donald will teach you how to build a successful life by owning your day. What you are about to read cuts the clutter and hits directly to the points that will change you forever.

This is not a 90-day plan. This is you living each day, one step at a time, to be the successful person you can be. If you have the will to take the first step, the daily practices you'll learn and employ will propel you through your day and help you to optimize your life.

Donald Burns is the real deal. He has insights from decades of interviews, studies, and practice in the restaurant industry. He has condensed many years into a simple tool. His authenticity and passion are shown daily with clients. He not only teaches it, but lives it regularly, and he shares it with you in this unique guide. It will not only change your mindset but will cause a paradigm shift in all areas of your life. Apply the lessons here, and you will see dramatic results!

Thax Turner
The ROI Life

TIME TO CHANGE YOUR MINDSET

LET ME ASK A QUESTION:

Do you want more? Maybe that's a silly question. However, I want to know if you want more from your restaurant and your life. It's okay if you're happy with what you have. It's also okay to want more. Wanting more goes against much of the mental conditioning that brainwashed us during our youth.

Do any of these statements sound familiar?

> *Be happy with what you have.*
> *Just be grateful.*
> *It could be worse.*
> *Don't rock the boat.*
> *Greed is bad.*

Yes? If your upbringing was anything like that of most people, you have been told that wanting more was irresponsible and wrong. Let me say that wanting more is human. You were designed to adapt and thrive. Society tells you to be happy with what you have. I'm here to tell you that you get what you dare to go after. We have a massive disparity between economic classes in the United States. You see it in the news all the time that the rich get richer and the poor get poorer.

Now, I am going to go out on a limb here and say that your mindset determines what you get from life. You've heard the stories of the person who, despite coming from economic setbacks (being on the "wrong side of the tracks"), struggling through school, and having pretty much the world working against them, they become a success story. How did they do it?

They developed an Outstanding Mindset.

Here's the good news: What one person can do; you can do too.

So, do you want more? Do you want to be more? If you say yes, then you need to be 100% fucking sure about it. If you only want more because it sounds good or you think it would be "nice," you'll never get it. I'm talking about an obsession that is burning like a fire inside your gut! You have to want it more than anything. Only then will to stand up and take action. Most people say they want more—few are willing to do what needs to be done to get it.

> *Would you sacrifice sleep?*
>
> *Would you give up wasting time watching 2-3 hours of TV each night!? Are you willing to get dirty and put in the real work?*
>
> *Are you willing to dump the bullshit stories you cling to that are keeping you stuck in the same day-to-day crap that gets you nowhere?*
>
> *Are you willing to listen?*
>
> *Are you committed to taking new actions to get new results?*

If you said yes that's a good start. But here's the truth behind that: Your words tell me what you say you want; your actions tell me what you are willing to do to get what you want. Talk is truly cheap.

It all begins with how you start your day. If you study success and peak performance as I do, you see that those who reach the top, those who overcome economic struggles, those who rise above the challenges that life likes to hand out like free lollipops at the bank are not lucky. They all set themselves up for success each day by doing certain things that ensure they win the day.

I want you to start to think in 24. You, me and every other living thing on this planet have just 24 hours each day. What you do with your 24 is the difference between success (getting more) and those who accept the life they have as it is. Time to move out of your comfort zone and into owning the experience you want. The successful don't accept things for the way they are or are "supposed" to be. No, it's time for you to bend reality to your fucking will. I have seen many do it. I've done it, and in this booklet, I will share with you how to achieve it as well. Hold on to your ass because shit is about to get real!

OWN TODAY

It all starts with committing to own the day. Take control of your 24. The past is a memory— you can't go back and change it. Tomorrow is just hope. What you control is right now. Like, today right now. Is shit going to pop up and try to throw you off your game? Hell yes. That is life's mission, to take your day and mess with you.

Would you be the person you are today without life throwing you a few curve balls? No way. When life throws you some curve balls in the future, I want you to swing at those fuckers like you're blindfolded and holding a lightsaber! You keep swinging until you make contact! That's how you beat life! That's how you get what you want!

Each day is a new 24. I want you to appreciate that gift. I want you to respect it. I want you to protect it. I want you to own it.

Here's how to do it.

BOOKEND THE DAY

How you start and finish your day is the most important concept I want you to learn to control. Yes, the day will get chaotic. The day will take unexpected turns and twists. Some days it will drop an F-5 tornado right on your happy and peaceful day. Remember that life is not going to give you a pass. The difference between those who get the restaurant and life they want is they don't submit or give up when life fucks with them. Sure, it might knock you down to your knees. Winners get back up, look straight into the storm of life and say, "You hit like a bitch. Is that all you got?"

So, to get ahead of the day, you're going to start strong and finish strong. No lazy start to the day! Remember when you open your eyes that the clock is ticking! If you sleep like most people, you are already 6-7 hours in a time deficit. You need to make up ground and start getting some shit done. Wasted time is wasted life. You have one life. You have one shot to leave a dent in the universe! Yes, a dent! Don't think small and just want to leave a mark. How average is that? Leave a dent!

PART I:
THE PRINCIPLES TO AN
OUTSTANDING DAY

BENDING TIME

Tick tock, tick tock. Time is one thing that people are always trying to manage, bend or wish they had more of. We all dream that time machines were real so we could finally control the uncontrollable. When you run a restaurant, time can either become your ally or an evil nemesis. Most people choose the latter and seem to fight with time continually.

So, how can you stop this love/hate relationship with time? Here are some simple ways to make time work with you and not against you.

Respect Time

Just like a lot of things in life, you need to give first to receive. Respect is a common theme in all relationships. Time is the same. You need to have a deep respect for your time and the time of others. One of the greatest gifts a person can give is their time. Remember, it can't be saved or traded. When you give your time and attention, you have given away a valuable and precious commodity. That's important to realize and respect.

It all starts with self-respect. You need to respect time for the gift it is. **You need to respect yourself.** You are powerful beyond measure if you can develop self-respect and make a sacred pact to honor it. Everything in your outer world first started in your inner world.

When people don't respect themselves, it becomes somewhat apparent in their behavior. Your words may say one thing; however, it's the actions you take that mean everything. This behavior will manifest in many ways. One of the most common is overcompensating behavior. That person who is loud, obnoxious, and demeaning to others? They quite often suffer from a lack of confidence and a lack of self- respect for themselves.

If people do not have respect for themselves, it's hard to get them to respect other things. This is an excellent interview question! Ask them point blank: ***"Do you respect yourself?"*** Then ask them to give you at least three examples of how they do that. You might be shocked that a lot of people get a blank look on their face when asked this question.

CONTROL FOCUS

You might see clever T-shirts that say "Time is Money." That's not true. Money can be saved; time cannot. So, time is not money; **money is money**. **Focus is the real currency.** How someone spends their focus is a mirror to what they value.

Watching TV for four hours a night is an ideal escape for a lot of people. Let's say they do this five nights a week—that's 20 hours. In a year, that's **1,040 hours**. Now, let's take it further and throw in the variable of your hourly worth. If you want to be worth more to others, you first need to be worth more to yourself. This goes right back to respect. So, let's say you want to make $100K a year. In an average

40-hour workweek, you would need to be worth $45.79 per hour to make that kind of money. Now, if you spent that time watching TV and put a dollar value on it, at the end of the year, you would need to pay out $47,621! *Ouch!* **I don't know too many people who would write a check out for $47K for watching TV.**

How do you take back control of your focus? Start being more selective about where you put attention and focus. The restaurant industry moves fast, and it's easy to get dragged into the demands it throws out at us. If you want better results, you need to ask better-quality questions. Here are some you need to ask:

- **Am I the best person to do this?** No, seriously. You don't need to do everything yourself. The people who are always doing everything are also the same people who love to play the martyr card. They don't respect or trust their team. ***Oh, and if you don't respect and trust your team, you don't** have a team— you have a one-person show with support.* That rarely works out. People like this either have a very high turnover or they bounce restaurant to restaurant, never finding profound, fulfilling success.

- **Who on my team could benefit?** Yes, think beyond your own needs. When you hold back giving your team a chance to grow, you are holding back the business. One of our human needs (not want, *need*) is to **contribute**. When you take control of everything and don't give others a chance to contribute, you'll soon see they stop asking for more responsibility. Next, you'll see their drive and motivation start to dwindle, too. After that, you have walking zombies working for you.

If you want to see where your time goes, conduct a time audit. Get a notebook and write down everything you do and how long you spend on each task for an entire week. This exercise can be a real eye-opener for most when you are brutally honest. We tend to think we get a lot done, but when we look back on the real data, it can be a little disheartening. To make a change, you first need to be aware of the habits that you've formed throughout your life. **Awareness precedes choice and choice precedes change**—if you make a conscious effort to take action and want to change.

RESULTS MATTER, NOT EFFORT

"I'm *so* busy!" That could be the battle cry for working in the restaurant industry. We're all busy. We're called **human beings** when in fact we should be called **humans doing**. Life moves quickly, and the human race is always pushing to be faster, better, stronger. What drives us is the need for more. It's not a bad thing to want to be better and wants more. The self-help industry is a multibillion-dollar conglomerate that fills that drive with books, audio, video, and workshops.

If you are not moving fast enough, you are quickly labeled by others as a "slacker." The issue is that we have concluded that being busy is the end goal. We think someone busy is successful. ***Not so fast!*** It doesn't matter how busy you are. Being busy for many people is a form of distraction.

They use it as a magician does: "Look over here and see how busy I am so you don't know what I'm doing." What matters is the results you get. Write this down:

> ***Never mistake being busy for being effective.***
> ***I'm rewarded for my results, not my effort.***

A line cook works a 10-hour shift and is moving really. He seems to have a lot of prep going. On the surface, you might think, "That cook is a workhorse!" They knocked out 4 four items on the prep list. Epic fail. It's not busy that matters. Sure, he stayed busy all day, yet when all is said and done, productivity was not that great. **Mediocrity loves to be disguised as being busy.**

PLAN THE DAY BEFORE

There is an old saying that goes, "Proper planning prevents piss-poor performance." Hands down the most effective tool for having a productive week is this: **Plan your work and then work your plan.**

We know that this business is fast-paced and demanding. It's easy to accept the status quo and say that you don't have time. However, what have we learned about owning time? You only own your attention and what you focus on. Your brain is wired to get you from want to want. Your mind is a problem-solving machine. That's why the questions you ask yourself tend to get you the results you ask for. Make poor queries, get poor results. If you ask, **"Why does this always happen to me?"** your brain will answer, **"Because you're an idiot."** Ask a better question like, "What is the lesson here, and how can I use that to be better?" *Seek, and ye shall find.*

Ideally, you want to tap into that problem-solving part of your brain to help you become more effective. That starts with having a game plan the day before. When you write down what you want and then decide on the actions needed to get the results you desire, amazing things happen. You start to get results.

So, could you eat an entire cow? Most would say, "No way." However, you could, **just one steak at a time**. The best thing to do is cut your day down into three tasks. Here's an economical system to get you started: index cards. You can pick up index cards at the store and start today. Take out an index card and draw a line down the middle. On one side, at the top, write "Task." On the other side, write "Action." Write down the three tasks you must accomplish for the day, the most important ones that can move you forward. These need to be big and bold. Remember:

> **"Dream no small dreams, for they have no power to move the hearts of men."**
> **-Johann Wolfgang von Goethe**

After you have your three tasks written down, in the next column, write down the next actionable task to move that forward. Most big dreams and goals can't be done with one or two actions. If they can, then you need bigger goals!

If you do this the day before and review it before you go to bed, your problem-solving brain will go to work. It will help you the next day when it comes time to get busy making things happen. Stacking the deck in your favor is always a smart move. Smart restaurant owners, operators, and chefs always have a plan.

DOES IT SEEM LIKE THERE IS NOT ENOUGH TIME?

It seems like we never have enough time in the day.

But what if you saw that you have plenty of time in the day? **86,400 seconds every day.** For some people that might seem like plenty. For others, that might seem like not enough. So how can some restaurant leaders get so much done every day? It all comes down to this: **Your relationship with time.**

Do you see time as out to destroy you? The answer to this question is quite revealing, and it's one you might want to explore. You will never learn how to bend time to your will unless you learn to respect time for what it is: **a valuable asset.**

Let's explore what time exactly is and is not.

UNDERSTAND THE FOUR TIME DIMENSIONS

The foundational core is understanding that you never really control time. It never stops. You can't call a timeout or hit a button to go back in time (not yet). Do you hear that tick, tick, tick on the clock? That's time telling you that it waits for no one.

So, what can you do? Like I mentioned before, you must control your attention and focus.

You see, there are four dimensions of time in which you spend various amounts of each day. Each of these dimensions wants your attention. Those that learn how to use time and not be used by it respect each dimension and allow only a certain amount of their precious 86,400 seconds every day to be allocated to each one.

	URGENT	NOT URGENT
IMPORTANT	**DEMAND**	**FLOW**
NOT IMPORTANT	**DELUSION**	**DISTRACTION**

DISTRACTION: This is the dimension that calls to you when you're stressed. Some might call it escapism. It could be something like watching that video on the Internet of the cat typing on a keyboard (which you've already seen 10 times), walking to the vending machine to grab a snack (even though you just had lunch 30 minutes ago), mindlessly browsing social media with no apparent intention (you might have gone on to post something and then got sucked into the rabbit hole), or asking Siri how much wood a woodchuck could chuck. If you spend most of your time in this dimension, you'll find that you're not living a life that people would call "inspired." *You're probably not very happy either.*

DELUSION: This is where the "busy people" tend to focus most of their attention. They always seem to have to-do lists that get longer and longer each day (without much progress). This dimension is very much like mental quicksand. The more you tend to fight, the deeper you sink in over your head. If you ever took 20 minutes to reorganize your desk or went through and organized those 1,000 emails sitting in your inbox (just so you'll feel like you've accomplished something), *welcome to the dimension of delusion.*

DEMAND: This is the **danger zone** for most restaurant leaders because many of the things that pop up in this dimension are critical to daily success in your business, and they do require your attention. Things will happen every day in the restaurant that require you to take action. The critical thing you want to ask yourself is the one mentioned earlier: ***"Are you the best person to take care of this?"*** The hard part for many is putting aside the **ego** that comes from spending too much time in this dimension. We all need to feel wanted and in demand, and it feels great to help others solve problems and issues. But when you spend too much of your time focusing on the demands of others and not enough on your own goals, you feel stuck on the hamster wheel of life. The biggest thing you can do to break free from this dimension is to understand the difference between being busy and being effective.

FLOW: This is the Promised Land. When you are in this dimension, you tend to lose track of time. Have you ever been so focused on an activity or around someone that you just became immersed at the moment? Like the chef who is so focused when he plates a dish that he doesn't hear all the noise around him in the kitchen for a few brief minutes. Or when you are having dinner with that special someone, and you're so focused on them that you don't realize the room is packed. **When you're in the dimension of flow, there is no past; there is no future, there is only the present moment.**

If you were to look back and reflect on your day, you would see a clear pattern of which dimensions you tend to spend your time in. The key to improvement in anything is self-awareness. Once you are aware of your pattern, you can make better choices. When you make better choices, your life and your restaurant will change.

Most managers seem to struggle with the dimension of demand, so let's talk about a few ways you can get control of this monster.

TRAIN YOUR TEAM TO SEEK SOLUTIONS

When you always solve the problems for your team, you take away their opportunity to become problem solvers. Think about it. Be honest: Did you know how to do everything you do in your current role without making a few mistakes? Of course not. Now, you might throw out, "It's from years of experience and developing good judgment." True. However, good judgment comes from learning from your mistakes. You need to allow your team some room to make mistakes. This doesn't mean setting them up for failure—it means letting them stretch their cognitive muscles to find solutions to problems. A leader in this role is more of a safety net and is there to offer assistance before they fail.

If your team is afraid to make decisions or approach you with a new idea, that's a reflection of you. You have built an imaginary wall—**built from fear**—that's holding your restaurant back from maximizing its potential. Trust builds teams and outstanding brands. Without it, you'll be stuck in a perpetual limbo of average, and **being average sucks**.

If you're clinging to the mindset that you must control everything and everyone, just know that you can't possibly control everything. **When you try to control everything, you control nothing that truly matters.** The tighter your grip on things and people, the more that slips away.

"The biggest lies we tell are the ones we tell ourselves."

So, if trying to control others doesn't work, what are you to do? The only thing in this world you control is you! Your thoughts, your beliefs, your reactions, and most importantly, your actions.

WRITE IT DOWN

It's understandable that if you work in the restaurant business, your life will move at a brisk pace. So fast at times that you think you can remember all the things that need to be done.

David Allen, the founder of the GTD (Getting Things Done) methodology, recommends getting things out of your head to a trusted place to remind you. His theory is that you only have so much psychic RAM or memory storage in your brain. It's far better to write things down and review them at least once a week.

Now, if you just write down all the things you need to do, you end up with an overwhelming to-do list. Let's not do that. Instead, when you need to write something down, you should ask yourself these questions to clarify and prioritize:

> *What is the result I want to get from this? What is the next action?*
> *Why is this important?*
> *Who is the best person to accomplish this? What is the deadline for completion?*

Let's take an example. Let's say you're working on a server training manual. The thought process would be like this:

Server Training Manual

RESULT: An updated, comprehensive training manual that instills our values and standards for the service team.

NEXT ACTION: Schedule a 15-minute meeting this Friday with the leadership team to discuss. **Why:** Consistent and constant training is the foundation for an outstanding guest experience. **Who:** Sally. She is excellent at turning training into high-energy learning workshops.

DEADLINE: First meeting this Friday. First draft in two weeks. The final training program in 30 days.

You see, when you ask better-quality questions, you get better results. *If you do not see the results you want, you need to ask yourself better questions.*

SCHEDULE IT!

People who have learned to bend time know that their calendar is their most valuable tool. **They schedule everything.** If you want to avoid those dimensions of time that tend to consume your attention, gain control of your calendar.

You must turn all the things you *should* do into *must*-dos. Maybe you want to join the gym and get in better shape. Why haven't you? Too busy? It's not that you're too busy, it's that you haven't made it a priority or asked yourself quality questions to discover *why* it's important to you.

The things that you *should* do rarely come together. They tend only to happen when all the conditions fall into place. When opportunity plus the right timing plus the proper resources align, "should" tends to happen.

Successful restaurant leaders don't wait for things to happen. They prioritize and ensure that tasks are accomplished by scheduling them on their calendar.

Here's the other secret about time: It doesn't care what you do with it. Time can be cold and heartless. At midnight, time starts a new day, with no real concern for whether you wasted or invested it; that's all up to you.

Ideas, thoughts, intentions, and lists of things to do are worthless if you don't get into action mode and make them happen. I will keep saying this until you get the concept: you don't control time, but you do control your attention and your focus. Sometimes, that requires self-discipline and the ability to prioritize the things you need to do during your day. That only happens when you take control of your calendar and schedule small blocks of time to work on the things that move you and your restaurant forward.

Distraction, delusion, and demands are continually trying to pull your attention in their direction. While it's impossible to ignore them all the time, you do have a say in how much of your time each day you are willing to give to them.

Again, there are 86,400 seconds in every day—that's all you get. You can't beg, borrow, or buy more. Your time and the time of others must be respected.

When you respect time and value it for what it is, then and only then will you be able to bend it to serve you.

PROCRASTINATION

People have been procrastinating since they first formed civilizations.

Figures such as Benjamin Franklin, Pablo Picasso, and countless others have spoken about how results and procrastination are mortal enemies.

Abraham Lincoln addressed procrastination in one of my favorite quotes on the topic:

> **"You cannot escape the responsibility of tomorrow by evading it today."**

What's truly strange when it comes to procrastinating is that we're all well aware that it's not going to help us. Many wear it like some fucking badge of honor: "I'm just a procrastinator." *So, what they're saying is that they're delaying action to a future date so as not to provide any value to anyone.*

Research has proven that procrastinators might feel better in the short-term but will suffer in the long- term.

The motivation behind procrastination doesn't matter much. Maybe someone is afraid of failure. Perhaps they think the pressure of a looming deadline helps them perform better. It doesn't matter.

What does matter is that procrastination doesn't come with results; *it comes with a price.*

Dianne Tice and Roy Baumeister conducted and authored a much-lauded study focused on the costs of procrastination, which was published in the *American Psychological Society* journal. They study finds that depression, low self-esteem, stress, anxiety, and irrational beliefs are all related to procrastination.

Not only does Tice and Baumeister's study reveal that procrastination is indicative of poor self- regulation, it finds that it's comparable to drug and alcohol abuse. It can't be dismissed as innocent or harmless behavior.

In other words, procrastination is extremely damaging.

The cost of procrastination is wasted time and the result every time, without fail, is that nothing is ever accomplished. Let's fix that!

CONQUERING PROCRASTINATION FOR GOOD

Those familiar with Tice and Baumeister's study, including myself, point to the following passage as its crucial takeaway:

> *"The present evidence suggests that procrastinators enjoy themselves rather than working at assigned tasks until the rising pressure of imminent deadlines forces them to get to work. In this view, procrastination may derive from a lack of self-regulation and hence, a dependency on externally imposed forces to motivate work."*

Rather than work on a given task, some people let their ego get in the way. They ignore or otherwise underestimate the importance of willpower and self-regulation. Instead of simply getting to work on a task to move things forward, they assume they can put it off because they overestimate their abilities.

If we're all honest with ourselves, we can admit that we overestimate our intelligence, willpower, and self-discipline. Who wants to think they are not a genius? That they're easily distracted? That they're lazy? Only a small percentage of us, if anyone at all.

Instead, most people blissfully see themselves as smarter than the rest with the ability to accomplish any task with ease. That is, until the time to put in actual work arrives. Suddenly, the procrastinators happily find any reason to put off the work. This failure in willpower, self-regulation, and self-discipline says, "Don't do that now. You have plenty of time. Relax. Have fun. Do something else. Anything else!"

Let me be clear that I'm not just talking about big tasks. Procrastinators aren't particularly concerned with whether a task is big or small—they just know they're supposed to do something. That's all it takes for their instinct to do, well, *nothing*, kicks in.

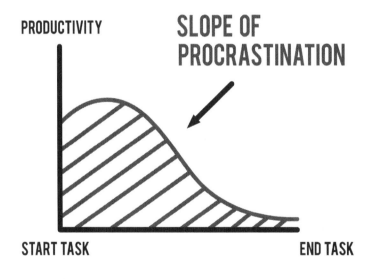

The graphic above, created by Darius Foroux, illustrates what he calls the "slope of procrastination." As he describes it, this slope occurs when, in between beginning a task and completing it, a person submits to a *single* distraction.

"And that's precisely the moment you give up being productive. You start working on a task, you're excited, you're focused, but then, after some time, you think: *Let's check out Facebook for a second,*" explains Foroux.

And that slope is just the beginning of a procrastinator's downfall.

A single distraction is a domino tumbling into its brethren. The procrastinator has already set aside their work to look at Facebook for "a second," so how about a quick visit to YouTube? An hour or two later, after they've fallen down a rabbit hole of YouTube videos, they may as well catch up on a few episodes of their favorite Netflix show…

Allow me to dispel any belief you have that procrastinators are unaware of what they're doing. They know about the cycle they find themselves in time after time. Their meaningless mantra? "I'll never waste my time again! Next time I'll nail it!"

If you believe that, let me tell you about an incredible opportunity for you to own a bridge I'm selling.

SYSTEMS WORK, NOT WILLPOWER

If you're an owner, operator, or chef, you likely didn't get into the restaurant business because you love rules. Well, you might love rules—those that you impose on your team.

Let me ask you this: **"Do you want to have freedom?"**

I don't mean the freedoms of a democratic society; I mean the freedom from rules, policies, and procedures. Asked another way, **"Do you dislike systems and routines?"**

Many in this business would answer yes to both of my questions. They think freedom is the ultimate measure of success. Well, procrastinators agree with that thought. They think they can accomplish tasks without having systems, procedures, or rules in place. Don't be like the procrastinators!

Instead, put rules against tasks—even if they're self-imposed, provided you have the discipline to stick to them—if you want to accomplish anything. Put the following together, and it creates a system that will help you accomplish any task:

Impose deadlines on yourself to create a sense of urgency. Create accountability through commitment with others (your business partner or partners, general manager, bar manager, etc.), so you learn to be more responsible and not let down your team. Break up your task into timed work intervals, so you don't lose focus and let the possibility of distraction creep in. Even committing to exercising for 20 or 30 minutes each day or imposing strict dietary restrictions on yourself can teach you to tackle tasks more effectively, not to mention both will give you more energy.

But arguably the best rule is to motivate yourself internally—nobody knows what motivates you as you do. And the best, simplest way to nail down your motivation is the following question:

Why are you doing this?

The best part of asking yourself that question is that doesn't apply only to the specific task on which you're working—it applies to everything you do in this business. Why are you doing this? Of all the things you could do, why the restaurant business?

Figure out you're why and you'll never grow bored or disengaged with tasks within your restaurant. You'll find that discovering your why in this business will carry over to the rest of your life and improve it.

TAP INTO SCIENCE TO MAXIMIZE YOUR POTENTIAL

My girlfriend is a badass scientist (I mean a real badass). What lights her up is when she is talking about her passion. If you listen to passionate people talk about what they love, it's contagious and inspiring. Great conversations get that one-pound piece of grey matter sitting on top of your head fired up with ideas. Then it hit me: Newton! *No, not fig newton's you food freak, Newton, the scientist.*

Way back in 1686, Sir Isaac Newton developed three laws of motion. The first law is often referred to as the **Law of Inertia**. The law states that every object will remain at rest or continue in a straight line unless compelled to change its state by the action of an external force.

In other words, things stay the way they are unless something comes along to disrupt them. This law has the power to make us or break us. And it is at work in your restaurant (and life) all day, every day whether you are conscious of it or not.

When we kick a ball down the field, it heads in a specific direction until it is acted upon by force greater than the force that is currently propelling it downfield. Like that ball, your restaurant is moving along a path that is taking you to a particular future, intentionally or not. And it will continue along that path to its destination until you do something different. It's not about what you want. It's about what you **are** doing. **Good intentions mean abso-fucking-lutly nothing.** It's a law, and as such, it is objective and indifferent to your good intentions.

Looking at this year, it'll be just like last year unless you exert a massively disruptive force to change your direction that is greater than the comfort zone you enjoy by continuing to do what you have always done - producing the same damn results again and again: **no extreme force, no extreme change.** Your days and years just repeat over and over and over again, just like a real-life version of Groundhog Day or what is known as a living hell.

If you're not where you want to be, change your direction with massive action. Get on a new path. New actions will produce different results.

Here's some good news: You can use another one of Newton's laws to your advantage. Newton's Third **Law of Motion**, which states that "for every action, there is an equal and opposite reaction." This could also be referred to as cause and effect.

If, for example, you were to jump off a tall building (the cause) the effect would be a sudden stop when you hit the ground! Falling itself isn't what kills you; it's the second part of the equation the effect that does...the stop.

For every cause, there is an effect. Today is connected to tomorrow. Every action you take and everything you say is taking you somewhere. You just need to be sure you're going exactly where you want to go; a path that is taking you to the person you want to become.

- If you work harder than you did last year, then you will do better.
- If you sacrifice now, then you are investing in our future.
- If you take time to read, then you will grow.
- If you improve your leadership, then people will follow you.
- If you are courageous, then you will inspire.
- If you are curious, then you will learn.
- If you avoid the trappings of the ego, then you will stay connected with those you serve.
- If you surround ourselves with the right people, then you will be enriched and will lift others.
- If you are authentic and humble, then you will build trust.

If you don't improve, then your circumstances won't improve either. You can't tell yourself that it's going to be alright if you are headed in the wrong direction. That's just bullshitting yourself, and we do it more than you think. Now life will naturally push you off-course and takes you on tangents. Anything meaningful in life is produced by moving upstream. You must fight against the current of mediocrity.

When you find yourself where you don't want to be, you must acknowledge the fact that you have drifted (oh, and we all do); you have gone with the path of least resistance. You'll need to make some course corrections...like now.

Believe me that we must make course corrections from time to time.

Of course, this implies getting uncomfortable. It's helpful to have a mentor, a coach, or a program that will keep us accountable, because we tend to say, "I worked hard today." (when if fact) we've barely touched our potential.

As we look at our life, we all have directions that need to be changed. It helps to begin this process by asking ourselves questions and giving serious (and honest thought) to the answers.

1. The big coaching questions I like to ask are:

- What worked for me last year and what didn't?
- What habits are holding me back?
- What three things do I want to accomplish next year?
- What is that one thing I need to accomplish this year?—your BAG—those Big Audacious Goals?
- What does an outstanding day look like?
- What routines keep me on track?
- Why do I do what I do?
- And most importantly, **what am I grateful for?**

If you can't answer these basic questions, then you are not focusing on the right things!

Now if you did, congratulations because you are in the 2% that takes action! Now it's time to drill down even more into specific areas of your life:

- Do I make time to study and feed my brain good stuff?
- What habits are draining my time and attention?
- What activities recharge me?
- Am I taking time to relax and grow in other areas of interest?
- Am I getting quality sleep?

- Am I eating healthy and avoiding processed crap foods?
- What do I need to change to my diet?
- Am I exercising regularly?
- Am I drinking enough water?
- Is my morning and evening routine setting me up for my best day?
- What strengths do I need to maximize?
- Am I where I would like to be in my work or career?
- How can I increase the value I bring to others?
- What relationships are building me up?
- Are any relationships taking me off-track?
- Are any relationships sucking the life out of me?
- Who do I take for granted?
- Do I support those around me?
- Do I support and encourage others?
- Do I focus on building others up?
- Do I make time for others?
- Where do I need to grow?
- What strengths do I need to improve on?
- What do I need to learn?
- What books do I need to read?
- What seminars do I need to attend?
- What can I learn from the mistakes I made in the past?

2. The key to moving forward is taking the first step forward.

Every destination needs a **M.A.P.** or what I like to think of as a **Massive Action Plan**! You need to know where you are and exactly where you want to go. Then you plot a course of action to get there. You cannot drive from LA to New York City in one day. You must make strategic stops along the way to hit your end goal.

What is the first thing you need to do to get you moving in the right direction? *It starts with how you start your day.*

PART II:
THE OUTLINE OF
AN OUTSTANDING DAY

MY OPTIMAL DAY

Now the following is what I have found works for me. You'll need to adjust this to your life and time. I do know that when I share this template for an **Outstanding Day** with others (*and if they apply it*), they all see dramatic positive changes to their lives.

Sometimes this timeline varies if I'm traveling for business. I still try to maintain the consistency of this format no matter what time zone I'm in. **Habits make and break the results you get.** If you're not getting the results you want, take a look at your habits and the choices you're making.

SLEEP IS CRITICAL

You need to sleep. Period. Sure, you can go for a few days without sleep if you have to. Once you pass your threshold, you'll start to get a little loopy. Go even further, and you risk going psychotic. In the military

Special Ops world, you go to a school called SERE School (Survival, Evasion, Resistance, and Escape).

Their primary tool to break you is sleep deprivation. Trust me that extreme lack of sleep makes people do things they normally would not.

I find that 7 hours of sleep is my optimal amount and my body's natural circadian cycle. I have run my sleep lab over the past year, and I set a standard time to get to bed. Now, I aim for 10:00 p.m. in bed (read for an hour) then lights out at 11:00 p.m. My body will naturally wake around 6:00 a.m. without the alarm clock.

Here are a few tips to optimize your sleep:

- **KEEP YOUR BEDROOM COOL.** Research has shown that around 67 degrees is best.

- **KILL THE ELECTRONIC DISTRACTIONS.** If you have a TV in your bedroom, take it out. If you like to read (like I do) before bed, ditch the iPad or Kindle and grab an old-fashioned book (yes, they still make them).

- **MOVE YOUR PHONE OUT OF YOUR REACH.** I got this tip from Mel Robbins, author of *The 5 Second Rule*. She doesn't have her cell phone near her bed, so it forces her to get up to turn the alarm off. I have been guilty in the past of being a habitual snooze bar hitter, and this new tip solved that issue pretty much overnight!

- **REHYDRATE.** As soon as you wake up, drink some water with fresh lemon. During sleep, you naturally get dehydrated because it tends to be the most extended period of the day where you don't drink anything. The lemon in the water will help your body get into an alkaline state fast.

- **BRUSH YOUR TEETH.** Your bacteria have been sitting in your mouth all night giving you a little dragon breath.

TAKE SUPPLEMENTS

Now fair warning—I take a shit load of vitamins and supplements. Once again, I find these work for me. **I'm not a doctor, so please check with your physician before adding anything new to your diet, particularly if you're taking medication.** Some things don't mix well, so be smart.

My Morning Vitamin List:

Aniracetam - 750 mg
Phenylpiracetam - 100 mg
Chromium Picolinate - 200 mcg
GABA - 500 mg
L-Tyrosine - 750 mg
Acetyl-L-Carnitine - 500 mg
Tri-3D Omega - 330 EPA/220 DHA

Dopa Mucuna - 15% L-Dopa
Rhodiola - 500 mg
5-HTP - 200 mg
Phosphatidyl Serine - 100 mg
L-Theanine - 200 mg
Active Adult 50+ Multivitamin
HPX OPTIMIZED Supplement by Brendon Burchard https://www.hpxlife.com/hpxsupplements

KETO DRINK

After taking my vitamins, I head for the kitchen for a drink to get my metabolism on the right track. I moved to a ketosis diet on the advice of my good friend, Thax Turner. There are entire books written about the subject. Here's the CliffsNotes version:

Ketosis is a natural state for the body during which it's almost entirely fueled by fat. This is normal during fasting, or when on a strict low-carb diet, a.k.a. The keto diet.

The "keto" in the word ketosis comes from "ketones," which is the name for small fuel molecules in the body. This is an alternative fuel for the body, produced from the fat we eat and used when blood sugar (glucose) is in short supply.

These ketones Ketones are produced when you consume very little carbs (the primary source of blood sugar), and modest amounts of protein since excess protein is converted to blood sugar.

When you stick to that type of diet, fat is converted to ketones in the liver and then enter your bloodstream. They are then used as fuel by cells in the body, just like glucose. They can even be used by the brain.

You can enter the state of ketosis by eating a ketogenic diet or undertaking a period of fasting.

When you're in ketosis, once the body's limited reserves of glucose begin to run low, your entire body switches its fuel supply to operate almost entirely on fat. Insulin (a fat-storing hormone) levels become very low, but fat burning increases significantly. The result? Faster, greater weight loss.

KETONES ARE BRAIN FUEL

One somewhat strange fallacy is the belief that the human brain requires carbs. The brain will and does burn carbs—if that's what you're eating. However, you don't have to worry about your brain if you don't eat a lot of carbs; your brain will burn ketones quite happily. The fact is your brain needs food to survive and function, and you don't have to feast on carbs to keep your brain happy. You need to eat to keep your brain happy and keep it from attempting to turn the proteins in your muscles into glucose. You wouldn't enjoy that—it means your body is going to waste away and waste away fast. So, yes, your brain wants food. No, it doesn't need to dine on large quantities of carbs.

Ketosis, as I'm sure you've come to realize by now, is the process that makes sure your brain can run on fat stores. I don't advocate you experimenting with this, but we've evolved to develop the ability to survive several weeks (possibly months) without consuming food. Our bodies—and brains—can survive on fat.

Again, I'm not a doctor, but the evidence suggests that you don't need to feed your brain carbs. Period.

Many people even feel more energized and focused when the brain runs on ketones, made from fat. It has worked wonders for my productivity and ability to focus.

Now, I cheat getting into ketosis faster by drinking a supplement in the morning. I use a product by Pruvit called Keto//OS (I like the orange dream flavor), and it's great because I can get the mix in individual packets which allows me to use it even with a busy travel schedule. If you would like more information or to give it a go, follow this link:

http://EA5GE8.DrinkYourSample.com

MEDITATE

Before you throw your hands up and assume I'm trying to brainwash you, let me say this:

No. I am not.

I want you to brainwash yourself.

I get hundreds of emails and messages on social media asking for tips to reduce stress, increase focus, and basically how not to be wound up as tight as a rubber band about to snap. **My answer: you need to meditate. *Start today!***

Don't just take my word for it. Here are some facts behind why you need to incorporate meditation into your morning routine if you genuinely want an **Outstanding Mindset**.

> *"The world we have created is a product of our thinking; it cannot be changed without changing our thinking." -Albert Einstein*

Developing a morning meditation practice will change your life. I am dead serious! We get all stressed out in this industry, and all we need to do to slow the damn world down is take some time each morning to slow our thoughts down. To meditate effectively, you must commit to the process and be patient along the way, as it is very challenging to slow

down and control your thoughts. You're going to get frustrated and will want to throw in the towel. Don't.

Here are four reasons you want to start and some tips on how to get going.

1. Start the Day Positive

It's easy to fall into the habit of hitting the snooze button to catch some extra z's or glancing at emails on your iPhone to start the day. However, when you go back to sleep, you usually end up feeling more tired than when you first woke up. And if you look at your phone, forget it; there goes your day. You start working, thinking about all the shit you have to do, and your mind starts its race of nonstop planning and organizing. Morning meditation will set the tone for your entire day and help you to be focused, content, and optimistic. Set aside 10 minutes a day first thing in the morning. If you say you don't have 10 minutes to improve your life by meditating, then you fucking need to sit your ass down and do this.

2. Calm Down

The mind tends to jump from one thought to another randomly, like a wild monkey jumping from tree to tree. In Buddhism, this concept is referred to as "monkey mind," but it's right for all of us who live in the modern world. By meditating and tuning into your breath and body when you first wake up, you become more aware of your thoughts–and that pesky monkey mind. One powerful benefit of meditation is being able to detach from habitual thought patterns, especially the negative ones. Through regular practice, you can gain control of your thoughts. Being in control in this way can help move you into a proactive state of being rather than a reactive one.

3. Prevent Stress

Numerous studies have suggested that meditation has various health benefits—most notably, easing stress. Meditation is a unique opportunity to create time for yourself, work deadlines, and other obligations. Although it isn't fully understood, researchers think that meditation may stimulate the parasympathetic nervous system, slowing your heart rate and breathing rate, and improving blood flow. These physiological effects that take place during meditation may be part of the reason why meditating makes you feel so relaxed. Beginning your day in a calm, relaxed state can also help you be less bothered by the little frustrations in life and reduce overall stress and anxiety. You'll be less likely to blow up on the girl at Starbucks for getting your order wrong! LOL

4. Boost Well-Being

Increased mindfulness makes us more emotionally stable and encourages a sense of wellness. Some evidence suggests that meditation might even boost immune function. Daily meditation practice will leave you feeling present each day, intensify your appreciation for positive experiences, and empower you in your life. **Hey, we all need a little more empowerment in our restaurant lives!**

HOW TO GET STARTED

- **GET COMFORTABLE.** Wear loose clothing and if you're cold, grab a blanket or shawl to keep warm. You want to be comfy so that you'll be able to focus instead of fidgeting.

- **CHOOSE A PLACE WHERE YOU WON'T BE DISTURBED.** If you can, dedicate a place in your home to be used only for meditation (I have a chair I use to meditate). Make this place your haven. If you like, personalize it with a candle, incense, pictures, or anything that you find calming. Use a blanket, block, or pillow so that you'll be able to sit comfortably with a nice, tall spine. This will help you stay alert while keeping your spine and legs at ease. Sit against a wall to support your back if necessary.

- **WATCH AND FEEL YOUR BREATH MOVE THROUGH YOU.** Focus on your third eye (the soft space in between your eyebrows) and take deep breaths. Just breathe and let your thoughts drift in and out of your mind.

- **BE INDIFFERENT.** Don't judge your thoughts. They are just thoughts. And besides, you get to choose what thoughts serve you, which ones to disregard, and how to act. Lucky you.

- **REMEMBER THAT MEDITATION IS A PRACTICE.** Some days will be harder than others. It's not about finding complete stillness in the mind but letting go of resistance and reactions to whatever arises. Morning meditation can be easy to blow off while lying cozy in bed, but once you've done it, keep in mind all the positive ways it makes you feel. Commit to your practice, and you'll see the benefits unfold. Last but not least, keep practicing.

I started meditating using apps on my phone. I have used both **Calm** and **Headspace** to get me into the **habit of meditation**. Try them out, see which narrator you like best, and get started today.

About a year ago, I was introduced to **TM** (Transcendental Meditation) by a good friend. You have to be taught TM by a certified instructor, and it does cost money to learn the techniques. However, I found it to be a worthwhile investment after using the meditation apps for a year, and I wanted to take my meditation to a new level.

You can learn more about TM from this link: https://www.tm.org/

WORKOUT

After meditation, I head to the gym. At first, I tried going at the end of the day. I found that I was usually exhausted and tended to come up with excuses about why I couldn't go.

It's late, and I still have some things to work on.

I'll just do extra tomorrow.

I didn't eat much today, so I'll be okay.

Yeah, we can all rationalize why we shouldn't do something.

With very little effort, you can talk yourself out of anything. ***I know I have.*** I will go out on a limb and say you have too.

Now, I don't make working out a *should*; I make it a *must*! I set my alarm far enough away from my bed that I must get my ass out of bed to turn it off. I also have my workout clothes ready and at the end of my bed. When I get up to turn off the alarm, I see the clothes (a trigger), and I say to myself, "Alright, I'm up—let's get this day going!"

Set yourself up for success by moving your alarm where you must get out of bed. Have your workout clothes and shoes ready. ***You need to change a few things to change your entire day!***

You don't have to go to an actual gym. You do, however, need to get in some exercise. Working in the restaurant industry can mean long hours. You might be on your feet a lot. You probably won't eat right and don't walk fast enough to get your heart rate up to gain any cardiovascular benefits. I know your pedometer says you walked 10 miles today, but your heart never got above 90 bpm, so no, you didn't work out.

PRIMING

If you follow my posts and have read my first book (Your Restaurant Sucks! Embrace the suck. Unleash your restaurant. Become outstanding.) .), you know I'm a Tony Robbins fan. His tapes and books helped me get through some tough times by replacing the negative self-talk within me with a positive inner monologue. All of us have ups and downs in life, so don't think that you're the only one. You're human— human beings have a range of emotions that we experience. That's life.

Those with an **Outstanding Mindset** don't avoid the highs and lows that emotions deliver. They don't get stuck when those emotions get low, dark, and depressing. **You have to respect the low emotions so you can truly appreciate the high emotions.**

I was fortunate to attend Tony Robbins' signature four-day event called **Unleash the Power Within** (UPW). During the four-day event (that goes 12-14 hours a day), you learn about what triggers your emotional responses. You learn to go beyond self-imposed limitations of the mind by walking on fire. You also learn how to recondition your brain with a morning routine called Priming. Below you'll find an example of Priming from Tony Robbins himself.

"Picture this: It's the morning, and you have no desire to get to work. You feel lethargic, apathetic, and frustrated – there's so much to do! You want to be focused and feel successful, but no matter how many cups of coffee you drink, you never feel fully energized. You only get a few things accomplished before calling it quits, setting yourself back, even more, the next day. *Sound familiar?*

When we're tired and down, it's hard to remember what achievement and success feel like. Luckily, there's a simple way to change your physical state and, with it, your state of mind."

What Does Priming Mean?

Several studies focused on understanding the power of priming have been conducted. One such study, which Robbins says illustrates the basics the best was conducted by researchers at Yale University. It went like this:

"In the elevator on their way to the lab, a member of the study team (who knew what they needed to do, but not why) would casually ask the participant to hold their coffee. The team member would then write down some information about the participant, then get their coffee back. Each participant would hold the cup of coffee for somewhere between 10 and 25 seconds. For half the participants, the coffee was hot, while the other half held cold cups of coffee. That's the only difference between the two groups of participants."

The next part is where things become truly intriguing:

"In the lab, all the participants read the same brief description of a person. They then rated this person's personality traits using a questionnaire. The people who'd held hot coffee for those few seconds in the elevator rated the person as more generous, happy, better natured, and more social than those who'd held cold coffee. People who'd held the cold cup were more likely to say the person they were rating was unhappy, irritable, and selfish."

If you recall, the profiles that both groups read had zero differences. It was the reactions between the two groups that differed, and they differed significantly. The most interesting and important element of this study is that neither group was aware they had undergone priming.

PRACTICE TONY ROBBINS' PRIMING EXERCISE YOURSELF

You don't have to put priming in the hands of chance; you can take control of it. Robbins' has listed the process of controlling your priming chance step by step. You'll find the steps below, along with an audio link of Robbins guiding you through his process.

10-minute Morning Priming

1. **SIT ACTIVELY:** Locate a chair in a (relatively) quiet area. Sit actively. This means placing both feet on the floor, shifting your shoulders back, chest up, and holding your neck long and your head high.

2. **BREATHE:** Changing your breath changes your state of being. Tony's method is a breathing exercise with three sets of 30 breaths, each with a pause in between each set. (1 minute)

3. **HEART BREATHING:** Put your hands on your heart and feel its power and strength as you breathe. (30 seconds)

4. **PRACTICE GRATITUDE:** Think of three things for which you're truly grateful in this moment. These three things can be from your past, your present, or your future. Create as clear an image as you can when thinking of the first thing. Make it so vivid and real that you "step into it" with your mind. Spend amount one minute on this image, then go to the second thing and then the third. Robbins suggests making *one of these three things simple, such as a child's smile or someone sincerely saying "thank you" to you.* (3 minutes)

5. **VISUALIZE:** Robbins likens this step to a blessing or prayer. He imagines colored light coming down and filling his body, healing whatever needs healing: body, thoughts, feelings, etc. Imagine that any problem you're experiencing is being solved. Ask for strength. (1 minute, 30 seconds)

6. **SHARE:** In this step, you send all your newfound energy, healing, and strength to others. Let yourself feel your energy being sent to everyone in your life: your family, your friends, your colleagues, your guests...even people you don't know but have encountered in your life. (1 minute, 30 seconds)

7. **FOCUS AND CELEBRATE:** Focus on three goals or outcomes you most desire. Go beyond wanting them and feel as though they've been achieved. Focus on that feeling and celebrate this sense of victory and completion. Picture how these three achievements are going to impact the lives of those who are around you. Treat this step in a similar manner to step 4, practicing gratitude. Feel success— experience it. (3 minutes)

8. **PREPARE TO TAKE ON THE WORLD.** Stretch your body, get out into the world, and tackle it!

I did this exercise every day for a year. When it came to the part where I was to visualize my outcomes, one was to be sitting at a table signing the first book I wrote. I imagined the orange cover and the gratitude from people saying they loved it. In December 2017, that vision became real, so I know this works!

Here is the link to the audio that will take you through the exercise by Tony himself: https://www.tonyrobbins.com/priming-exercise/

THE BIG 3

Next, I pull out my Big 3 Card and look at the only three things I must focus on for today. That's it, just three. Trust me, if you can get three things done that are important to you, that will place you further ahead than most people. When you focus on three things, they no longer seem overwhelming. That's the goal. Think of your life as a big chunk of marble. You don't just start chipping away and have a beautiful sculpture in only one day. Make a little progress (consistently) each day, and eventually, you'll have a masterpiece.

LEVELUP!

FEELINGS FOR THE DAY:

PERSONA:

TO BE COMPLETED BY

BIG 3

I MUST

You can also see that there's a place for one Must on my card. This is one item that I must complete, no matter what. For this to work, do what I do and put that kind of weight on one task, so it has urgency and importance. Our instinct is to fight the urgent and ignore the important. Plus, working in the restaurant industry isn't like working in any other business. You'll find that other people will come at you and try to give you their problems, particularly if you're in a leadership role. I kindly refer to this as **"others throwing their monkeys onto to your back."** Keeping your card to just the Big 3 and one Must make the chance of you getting important things done much more realistic. *(I teach my full system of Peak Productivity at The Restaurant Coach™ University in the course called LevelUP!)*

Then I make sure my calendar is fully booked for the day. **I find that white space on your calendar is the enemy of owning your 24 and getting results.** Other people will demand your time, and if you don't have your day planned out, they'll take time from you. **If you don't have chiseled out time to move your life forward, then you don't have a life!** Instead, you're living in the dimensions of demand, delusion, and distraction. You don't work on your 24; you're just sitting on the sidelines letting life pass you by.

> *If you need a wakeup call to get control of your life and your restaurant, this is it.*

Stop playing small in the world. It starts with creating an **Outstanding Mindset** and **owning the next 24 hours**. Start with that and just focus on the next 24.

WHAT ARE YOU DOING WITH
YOUR 24?

YOU GET THE LIFE YOU HAVE THE COURAGE TO GO AFTER.

MY #1 PRODUCTIVITY TOOL
– THE ALARM NUDGE

Next, we're going to use another great feature that's already built into your smartphone: the alarm feature. How are you going to use it to keep you on task and on target throughout the day? You're going to use your alarm as a gentle nudge.

You want to set at least five reminders throughout the day. I've personally used this system since 2009, and I have seven reminders through the day that keep me dialed in.

You'll see in the picture I have one at 9:00 a.m., 11:00 a.m., 1:00 p.m., 3:00 p.m., 4:00 p.m., 6:00 p.m., and 9:30 p.m. (yes, I work late). Every time the alarm goes off, it asks me a straightforward question: **What's Next?**

Now through the years, some of the questions have been modified to include:

- **Remember your Big 3! Get focused!**
- **Be aware of distractions; control your attention.**
- **Focus is your currency. How are you spending yours?**
- **Are you focused on the important or just goofing around?**
- **What more can you do?**
- **When would NOW be a good time?**
- **Focus! Focus! Focus!**

And my favorite:

- **What's Next?**

This alarm system is a great way to train your brain. I've used it for so long that I barely look at my watch anymore and go by when the alarms go off. ***Try it—I think you'll like it.***

HOW I END THE DAY

Around 9:30 p.m., you'll see I have an alarm that goes off on my phone telling me it's "**Time to start shutting it down!**" I can get lost in a flow while working on projects or writing, so this is my little reminder—my nudge—to myself to start turning off the computer and start my evening routine.

Here's my routine:

- **Power down** and turn off computers, iPads, and other electronic devices

- Fill out my **Big 3 Card** for tomorrow. Our brain is truly a problem-solving machine. I find I achieve the best results and have the most productive days when I do my Big 3 Card at night before I go to bed. That way, my unconscious mind is already starting to connect the dots and help me hit the ground running in the morning.

- Set my phone alarm and place it on the charger in my bathroom.
- Brush my teeth.
- Drink a glass of water.
- Clean my face and put on moisturizer *(don't judge, I'm getting old!)*
- I think of **three things (people) I am grateful for from the day** and I let that positive energy flow through my body.
- I'll read a book (like a real physical book) for 30-45 minutes. I keep an old-fashioned notebook by my bed to write down any ideas or thoughts that come from reading. **NO ELECTRONICS IN BED!**
- Lights out and goodnight!

WANT MORE?

School is never out for the true professional. If you have applied the principles outlined in the booklet, you will see some fantastic results. The beautiful thing about getting a taste of success is you want more!

Welcome to **The Outstanding Mindset Club**! You can go over and join the **Private Facebook Group – Outstanding Mindset Book** for like-minded people like yourself who have made it through this book and wanted to network with others that want more from themselves and their restaurants. You are the result of the people you associate with regularly. The Facebook Group is your place to find peers that will lift you to become your best! **Plus, I have some wicked bonuses available for you in the group as well.**

Hey, it's free to become a member since you purchased the booklet. *When opportunity knocks, you have to do your part and open the damn door.*

You will have to do the work and apply the principles in this book to get results. Many will get this book, read it, and not do one thing new to get the life they want. I am betting you are not like that. You will take action, and you will get results. Just make sure to create new habits and to keep on yourself. Change is never easy. If it were, everyone would have the life and restaurant they want...*we know that most don't.*

The Restaurant Coach™ Podcast is another *free* resource that you just need to subscribe to so you never miss an episode. Interviews with leading restaurant experts, tools, and tips to get you the restaurant and life you want.

THE RESTAURANT COACH™ (TRC) NATION

"A lot of people put pressure on themselves and think it will be way too hard for them to live out their dreams. Mentors are there to say, 'Look, it's not that tough. It's not as hard as you think. Here are some guidelines and things I have gone through to get to where I am in my career.'" — Joe Jonas

I started **TRC Nation** as a place where sisters and brothers from the restaurant industry could gather to get solutions to real issues they face every day. Not a place to bitch and complain about how much the industry sucks, but a place where positive attitudes prevail. I truly love this industry with all my heart, and if you become a member of TRC Nation, you do too, even if you might have fallen out of love with it.

The spirit of hospitality is what drives us, and I wanted to help bring that back to the restaurant world. To do that I wanted to **start** a **mentoring** program for restaurant leaders (at all levels) **to start** the revolution to bring back the core values that the restaurant world once had: respect, integrity, compassion, humility, and service to others.

TRC Nation is honored to have a growing list of world-class industry experts (mentors) that are willing to donate some time each week (for an 8-week program) to help others rekindle that spark and find direction in a turbulent industry.

Each mentor has been hand-picked by myself for the experience they offer and the value they bring every day to raise the standards in the restaurant industry.

How do you get a mentor? It's easy. First, apply to join **TRC Nation on Facebook** and then apply to get a mentor from the post talking about the program! Just hit **'Sign Up'** and the road to getting everything you want begins! See you inside TRC Nation!

https://www.facebook.com/groups/135011193999569/ mentorship_application/

GET AN ACCOUNTABILITY PARTNER ... THAT MEANS A COACH!

Do you have a coach?

If not, you could be limiting your restaurant's success. That's because coaches help you identify and focus on what's important, which accelerates your success. Great coaches:

- **Create a safe environment in which people see themselves more clearly;**
- **Identify gaps between where the client is and where the client needs or wants to be**
- **Ask for more intentional thought, action and behavior changes than the client would have asked of him or herself**
- **Guide the building of the structure, accountability, and support necessary to ensure sustained commitment**

Successful athletes understand the power of coaching. The United Kingdom Coaching Strategy describes the role of the sports coach as one that *"enables the athlete to achieve levels of performance to the degree that may not have been possible if left to his/her endeavors."*

Innovative restaurant brands understand that coaching can help their leadership team increase their performance at work. They invest in coaching for their senior leaders and high potential employees

Coaching also has an impact on an organization's financial performance; according to an International Coaching Federation study, 60% of respondents from organizations with strong coaching cultures report their revenue to be above average, compared to their peer group. Coaching pays for itself when applied.

If you are starting a restaurant and want to set yourself up for success right from the start or if you are an existing restaurant that wants more... coaching is the ultimate tool.

Now is coaching for everyone, of course not. Visit my website at **www.therestaurantcoach.com** to learn more.

> **Restaurant coaching is not for everyone. Side effects include increased profits, better staff, happier guests, stronger brand identity, reduced stress, improved relationships, and quality sleep. Talk to The Restaurant Coach™ to see if coaching is right for you.*

ABOUT DB

Donald Burns is The Restaurant Coach™, named one of **The Top 50 Restaurant Experts to Follow and one of 23 Inspiring Hospitality Experts to Follow on Twitter**. He is the leading authority, speaker, and international coach on how restaurant owners, operators, and culinary professionals go from just **good** to becoming **outstanding.** A former USAF Pararescueman (PJ), restaurant owner, and Executive Chef with Wolfgang Puck has the unique skills to break restaurants free from average and skyrocket them to peak performance. He works with restaurants that want to **build their brand**, **strengthen their team**, and **increase their profits** without sacrificing their lives to their business.

He is the author of:

Your Restaurant Sucks! *Embrace the suck. Unleash your restaurant. Become outstanding.*

Your Restaurant STILL Sucks! *Stop playing small. Get what you want. Become a badass.*

Pick up your copy at Amazon!
Available in Kindle and Paperback Formats.

ACKNOWLEDGMENTS:

I could not do the things I do (or would be the person I am today) without the support and encouragement from some fantastic people in my life who elevate me and encourage me to become my best:

Catherine Christoffersen, Thax Turner, Donna Turner, Kelly Musselman, David Klemt, John Trevor-Smith, Byron Kelly, Jay McCarthy, Kelley Jones, Eva Ballarin, and Brian Duncan.

> *I am grateful for each of you.*
> *Tashi Deley*

Author's Note: When people in Tibet greet one another, instead of saying "Hello," they press the palms of their hands together, hold them in front of their heart and say, "Tashi Deley" - which means, "I honor the greatness in you. I honor the place in you where lives your courage, honor, love, hope, and dreams."

Made in the USA
Middletown, DE
12 July 2019